The Inspirational Story of Football Superstar J.J. Watt

Table of Contents

Introduction

As the title implies, this is a book about [The Inspirational Story of Football Superstar J.J. Watt] and how he rose from his life in Wisconsin to become one of today's leading and most-respected football players. In his rise to superstardom, J.J. has inspired not only the youth, but also fans of all ages throughout the world.

This book also portrays the struggles that J.J. had to overcome during his early childhood years, his teen years, and until he became what he is today. A notable source of inspiration is J.J.'s own foundation that was named after him, as well as his consistent support of other charitable organizations. He continues to serve as the humble, mild-mannered superstar in a sport that glorifies flashy plays and mega personalities.

Combining impressive size, overwhelming athleticism, soft hands, and superior coordination, J.J. has shown the ability to impact a game in a variety of ways. From being a young athlete who could play multiple sports to becoming, perhaps, the most destructive defensive player of his generation, you'll learn how this man has risen to the ranks of the best football players today.

Thanks again for grabbing this book. I hope you are able to take some lessons from J.J.'s life and apply them to your own!

Chapter 1:

Youth & Family Life

The world welcomed Justin James Watt on March 22nd, 1989. He was born in Waukesha, Wisconsin to father, John, and mother, Connie. J.J. would be the first of the three children in his family. His father was a firefighter and his mother was a building operations vice president. He has two younger brothers, T.J. and Derek, who are six and eight years his junior, respectively.

J.J. would show athletic promise as a youngster, as his physical dominance was obvious from a very young age. He became interested in a variety of sports, including football, basketball, baseball, and hockey. J.J. has stated his favorite sport growing up was hockey, and he played it all the time from about the age of 3 to 13. Because hockey was also the most expensive sport of the ones he enjoyed playing, his family decided the travel and new equipment costs were taking a toll on the family's disposable income. J.J. then quit hockey and continued to thrive in the other sports he loved, specifically football.

Although hockey was his first love, J.J. was a huge football fan, even during his younger years. Growing up in Wisconsin, he became a huge fan of Reggie White and the Green Bay Packers. When he was 7, J.J. told a local paper that he idolized Reggie White, and that he wanted to be a good football player someday. He went to pep rallies and watched the players and the cheerleaders. He shared this dream with his parents and his elementary teacher, Mrs. Keith.

J.J. continued being a multi-sport athlete when he attended Pewaukee High School. He lettered all four years in football, as well as lettered twice in both basketball and baseball, and once in track and field. On the football field, J.J. initially played the tight end and defensive end positions. Because of his great footwork and agility, J.J. was able to run routes and catch passes on offense. However, because he also possessed great physical strength and power, his abilities on the defensive side of the ball were too much for his coaches to pass on.

J.J. would go on to catch 26 passes for 400 yards and even score six touchdowns as a senior. While on the defensive side of the ball, he was able to register 10 total sacks, 70 total tackles, 5 forced fumbles, 4 recoveries, and an all-time school record of 22.5 tackles for loss. Because of this impressive season on the gridiron, J.J. was honored with the Woodland Conference Player of the Year award, as well as voted to the All-Woodland Conference first team - for both the defensive end and tight end positions. To top his list of accolades for the season, J.J. was also named as the *Milwaukee Journal Sentinel* Athlete of the Year.

While he also shined on the basketball court, the baseball diamond, and in track and field, J.J. was convinced that he had potential to make it big on the football field. He was a great shot putter for his high school team - even winning the 2007 State Championship, but nowhere near the prospect that he had become on the edge of an offensive and defensive line.

By the time J.J. had ended his senior year at Pewaukee High School, he was ranked as only a two-star recruit by Rivals.com. However, the most impressive factor that J.J. had going for him was the fact that he was the seventh-highest rated prospect in the entire state of Wisconsin. He went on to visit the University of Minnesota, the University of Colorado, and Central Michigan University. By the end of his recruiting process, J.J. committed to play football for the latter.

Chapter 2:

College

J.J. arrived at Central Michigan University with high expectations, and he was slotted into the tight end position from the get-go. He went on to catch eight passes for the season, resulting in 77 total yards. However, by season's end, J.J. was not sure of the direction that both he and the football program were heading. He decided that he was best served to transfer from Central Michigan University to the University of Wisconsin.

Upon transferring to the University of Wisconsin, J.J. decided to redshirt his first season at the school. While he was redshirting, J.J. spent time developing his body, learning the team's plays and schemes, as well as developing chemistry around his teammates. He went into the following year, ready to contribute to the Badgers football team.

At the beginning of his time at the University of Wisconsin, J.J. and the coaching staff decided that he and the team would benefit from him committing to the defensive side of the ball full-time. He was assigned to play the defensive end position in his second year with the program. He went on to thrive in the role, finishing his first playing year with 44 tackles and four sacks.

J.J. used the off-season to take his game to the next level, as he trained hard and honed in on what it meant to be an elite defensive end. His hard work paid off by the time the season came around, as he finished with almost 60 tackles, seven sacks, two fumble recoveries and even an interception. This dominance on the defensive side of the ball allowed his teammates to break free whenever he would get double teamed. Furthermore, it allowed the defensive backs behind him to play a bit more aggressively, because they knew the quarterback would be under pressure.

Thanks to a well-coached team and a balanced attack on offense and defense, the team was able to have a very successful season. They went on to make the 2011 Rose Bowl, but lost to Texas Christian University in a hard-fought game.

By season's end, J.J. had become a priority on any opposing team's scouting report of the Badgers. He was receiving national attention by fans, as well as scouts from the National Football League. J.J. was honored for his efforts in his second season with the University of Wisconsin when he won the Lott Trophy and was a finalist for the Ted Hendricks Award. Both of these feats are a big deal for players at the collegiate level because of the prestige of past winners and what they have gone on to accomplish at the next level.

Because of J.J.'s hard work and preparation, combined with the hype that was surrounding him as a prime defensive prospect, he and his family decided he would be best served to forego his senior season at the University of Wisconsin. In early January of 2011, J.J. announced that he would be entering the 2011 NFL Draft.

Chapter 3:

Professional Life

J.J. was listed as one of the top defensive lineman in the entire 2011 NFL Draft, but it was not certain that he would get drafted in the first round. The Houston Texans were keen on J.J. and found his combination of speed, power, and technique to be just what they were looking for in a pass rusher.

In hopes to take their defense to the next level, the team drafted J.J. as the 11th overall selection in the first round. The Texans would not wait long before committing to their new defensive prospect, as they signed him at the end of July to an $11 million contract that covered the span of four years. He was also given a signing bonus of over $6 million as well.

At the time of the draft, many football experts believed that J.J. was a perfect fit within a 4-3 defense. But, he quickly showed that he could also be a dominant 3-4 end. He is intelligent, hard-working, and determined. He does not necessarily possess initial quickness, but he closes fast and hard on the quarterback. He also has enough straight-line speed to chase the ball from the backside. He has fast hands and good height. This combination of factors allows him to potentially bat down several passes per game.

First Season

J.J. showed great promise during training camp, as well as in the Texans' preseason games. Because the team did not have a designated starter heading into the season, J.J.'s abilities were able to earn him the starting role of defensive tackle/defensive end for the team.

His first regular season game with the team gave the coaching staff confidence in their decision, as J.J. went on to record five solo tackles in the game to go along with a big fumble recovery. He continued to post solid outings as the season progressed and showed he could be a key player for the Texans heading into the off-season.

His season totals consisted of 56 tackles (48 solo), 5.5 sacks, 4 passes defensed, two fumble recoveries, and even a blocked field goal. This wide range of statistics showed J.J. possessed a variety of skills that could benefit the team. Not only was he becoming an emerging pass rusher, but he was also showing that his coordination and intuitive timing allowed him to batt down balls at the line of scrimmage - a rare combination for defensive lineman. Furthermore, his leadership on and off the field were integral in the confidence of the defensive unit on a week-to-week basis.

The Texans went on to make the AFC Playoffs, in large part, due to their exceptional defense. In the team's first-ever postseason game against the Cincinnati Bengals, J.J. was able to make a game-changing play as he intercepted Bengals' quarterback, Andy Dalton, and returned it all the way back for a touchdown. This pick six was the first of J.J.'s career and his first NFL touchdown. The play came right before halftime and gave the Texans a 17-10 lead. It changed the momentum of the game, and the Texans were able to capitalize on the halftime lead, finishing the game with a 31-10 score.

The win advanced the Texans to the second round, where they would face the Baltimore Ravens. The team was unable to beat the heavily-favored Ravens, but the game was closer than many experts had predicted. Personally,

J.J. continued his excellent postseason play by sacking Ravens' quarterback, Joe Flacco, 2.5 times and put pressure on him throughout the game.

The 2011 postseason did wonders for J.J.'s popularity amongst fans, especially those in Texas. His exciting game-changing plays were something that fired up fans looked forward to each game. Furthermore, J.J. had become one of team's most impactful defensive players by the end of the year.

Second Season

Despite the built-up praise that J.J. was receiving before his sophomore season with the Texans, he used the off-season to really take his game to the next level. He was not satisfied with his progress - a theme that continues to show itself in J.J.'s life - and wanted to impact the team even more than he did in his rookie campaign. After the departure of his running mate, Mario Williams, from the defensive line, J.J. was counted on to become the anchor up front for the team.

By Week 12, J.J. had already broken the Houston Texans franchise record for most sacks in a single season. He broke former teammate, Mario Williams', record in the Thanksgiving game against the Detroit Lions. By season's end, J.J. recorded 81 tackles (69 solo), 20.5 sacks, four forced fumbles, 2 recoveries, almost 40 tackles for a loss, and an insanely high total of 16 passes defensed.

These incredible statistics put J.J.'s season in the history books as one of the best years that any defensive lineman has ever had. His ability to swat down passes was truly special to watch, so much so that he received the nickname "J.J. Swatt" by football legend, Jon Gruden, because of his ability to batt down balls consistently. To put it in perspective, J.J. had more passes defensed than many defensive backs around the league. He also became the first player to ever have a season with more than 16.5 sacks and 15 tipped passes.

The team performed well for the season, getting back to another AFC Playoff appearance. They were matched up with the Cincinnati Bengals in the Wild Card round for the second consecutive season. J.J. showed that he loved the big moments, once again, as he posted 5 tackles and a sack for the game. The Houston defense was able to hold the Bengals to only six offensive points for the entire game, and the Texans advanced with a 19-13 victory.

Waiting for the Texans in the second round was the powerhouse New England Patriots, the second ranked team in the AFC. The Texans' defense was not as good as it was in the previous game, giving up a total of 41 points.

However, it was far from only a defensive shortcoming, as the Houston offense struggled to score on the Patriots defense. J.J. was still able to make four tackles and was credited with half a sack for the game.

J.J.'s incredible sophomore season was recognized around the league. He finished the year as the AFC Defensive Player of the Year, as well as the AP NFL Defensive Player of the Year - receiving 49 out of a total of 50 votes. The season also marked his first as a Pro Bowl player, when he was chosen as the starting defensive end for the AFC Team in the 2013 Pro Bowl. Not surprisingly, J.J. was also chosen as a member of The Associated Press All-Pro team.

As mentioned earlier, his season would go down as one of the greatest by a defensive player ever, and J.J. was quickly becoming one of the most popular and fan friendly stars in the game.

Third Season

During the off-season, J.J. was named to the NFL's Top 100 list as the number five player in the entire league. Not only was it the highest that a defensive player had ever been ranked, but it was also the highest a player had debuted. He entered the season as every offensive coordinator's main focus when the Texans were the opponent. He was also allowing his teammates to be more successful, because he was drawing double teams on a regular basis.

Amazingly, in many instances, J.J. was able to get to the quarterback after being double and even triple-teamed. For the year, J.J. recorded 80 tackles, 10.5 sacks, 7 passes defensed, four forced fumbles, and two recoveries. However, his efforts did not lead to team success, as the Texans finished the year with a 2-14 record that was the worst in the entire National Football League.

J.J. would be named to the AFC Pro Bowl team for the second straight season and was still considered as the best defensive player in the game. It should be noted, as a normal occurrence in the progression of a star defensive lineman's career, statistics usually drop after a break-out season. This is rarely a case of the player's abilities regressing, but rather the change in defensive schemes he faces. Just like in J.J.'s case, most offensive coordinators instruct their teams to at least double team a force like J.J. This is the reason J.J.'s impact cannot be completely measured by statistics, because when he is double-teamed, his teammates benefit.

After J.J.'s third season in the league, the Texans knew they had a bona fide superstar and wanted to show they appreciated his efforts. The team offered him a $100 million contract, covering the span of six years. The deal also included over $50 million in guaranteed money - the most ever for a defensive player in the National Football League. Additionally, his annual salary of almost $17 million was the highest ever for a defensive player, representative of the impact J.J. was making out there on the football field.

During his third season, many football analysts began pointing out that J.J. was so good that he still beats his opponents, even when they have the upper hand in positioning. He gained a reputation of being a "beast" on the field. Ravens tight end, Owen Daniels, said in an interview that J.J. does everything that he can do on a daily basis to make himself better at football. He said that J.J. centers all his life decisions around his desire to be a better football player, even down to the toothpaste he uses. Daniels said he did not see any better defensive end than J.J. Watt.

Fourth Season

J.J. continued his rise to football superstardom in his 4th season in the NFL. It came as a surprise to many when he was nominated for MVP of the league. It had been 29 years since a defensive player was named MVP. In fact, there has not been a defensive player who has gotten as many MVP votes as J.J. since 1999. He received 13 votes, while Aaron Rodgers earned the MVP award with a 31 vote total.

Through 15 games that season, J.J. compiled 72 tackles, one interception, and 17.5 sacks. He also had five fumble recoveries, three forced fumbles, and five touchdowns! At this juncture, he became the highest paid non-quarterback in the league.

He scored his second touchdown during a game against the Buffalo Bills on September 28th, 2014. He picked off a pass from E.J. Manuel that was intended for Fred Jackson, and returned it 80 yards for the touchdown. This is the 4th longest interception return in the history of the Houston Texans franchise. Furthermore, J.J. hit E.J. Manuel nine times during the game.

J.J. was named the AFC Defensive Player of the Month for September 2014. During a game against the Indianapolis Colts on October 9th, 2014, J.J. forced Andrew Luck, the Indianapolis Quarterback, to fumble. He recovered the ball and returned it forty-five yards for the touchdown.

During a game against the Cleveland Browns, J.J. caught a 2-yard pass from Ryan Mallet, the Texans quarterback, and earned his fourth touchdown of the season. This was the first touchdown pass in Mallet's entire career. Watt also had one assist tackle, 4 solo tackles, one forced fumble, one sack, and a fumble recovery in the same game.

He scored his fifth and final touchdown on November 30th, 2014 after catching a one-yard pass from Texans quarterback, Ryan Fitzpatrick. J.J. became the first defensive player to score at least 5 touchdowns in one season since 1944.

In a game against the Baltimore Ravens on December 21st, J.J. recorded his 54th sack. He then broke the record of Mario Williams as the franchise leader in sacks. J.J. posted 3 sacks in one game on December 28th, 2014, against the Jacksonville Jaguars.

Because of this outstanding season, J.J. was named as the defensive end of the 2014 All-Pro First Team, as well as the defensive tackle of the 2014 All-Pro Second Team. He was also included in the 2015 Pro Bowl game. He was part of Team Carter, where team captain, Chris Carter, chose J.J. as captain of the defense. J.J. recorded an interception and a fumble recovery during the game. He was also named the Defensive MVP of the Pro Bowl. To top the season off, J.J. also won the Defensive Player of the Year award for the 2014 season.

J.J.'s fourth season was his best yet. He totaled 20.5 sacks and also had five fumble recoveries and the incredible five touchdowns! This season helped strengthen his status as a football superstar and showed that his dominance on the defensive end was irrespective of any scheme, luck, or strategy. Plain and simple, J.J. was now one of the best football players in the entire league - regardless of position.

Fifth Season

As of this writing, J.J. is the leading contender for the Defensive Player of the Year award for the third time in his short career. He was unanimously chosen as the defensive end for the 2015 NFL All-Pro Team.

While his statistics have dipped a bit from his fourth season, J.J. is being met with double-teams nearly every game. However, J.J.'s impact goes far beyond the numbers. The constant pressure that he applies at the line of scrimmage allows for his teammates to break through and blow up plays because of ample opportunities.

As a true testament to J.J.'s greatness, in July 2015, the NFL hailed J.J. as the number 1 ranked player in the league, besting seasoned veterans like Aaron Rodgers and Tom Brady.

Aside from the admiration of Texans fans and football analysts, J.J. also earned the respect of his colleagues. Robert Mathis said in an interview that he has full respect for Watt. "He can break the game. Guys like that, you call them a menace." Indianapolis Colts linebacker, D'Qwell Jackson, also called J.J. "a hell raiser".

Chapter 4:

Personal Adult Life

As mentioned earlier, J.J. is the type of player, who is never satisfied with previous success. He works hard each day to earn his money and doesn't treat this stardom he has received as something to be taken lightly. As an example, he wakes up at 3:45 a.m. daily to exercise and train.

He does his best to serve as a positive role model both on and off the field, being a humanitarian and philanthropist in the communities he is around. Furthermore, he has also settled nicely into Houston and has become one of the city's most known celebrities.

He has starred in many commercials, both locally and nationally - including commercials for H.E.B. He has endorsement deals with companies such as NRG Energy, Reebok, Gatorade, Verizon, Ford, and Papa Johns. He is also part of Reebok's "Be More Human" advertising campaign.

His personality and playing style makes Texans, specifically Houstonians, proud that he represents their organization. Even though he is a Wisconsin native, he enjoys the Texan culture and has been able to integrate into it nicely.

His younger brothers are currently both student athletes at his alma mater, the University of Wisconsin. Both brothers play football and would love to follow the footsteps of their older brother. J.J. still loves his Wisconsin roots and visits the area often. He is a very loyal person, who doesn't get caught up in trends and new faces. He enjoys a simple lifestyle and interacting with youngsters, who love the game, because of the passion that they have, instead of any monetary incentive.

To his many fans, J.J. Watt is a real life action hero. He is a full-fledged celebrity, as he's been asked to appear at bar mitzvahs, graduations, and weddings. He has been asked to be the commencement speaker of many colleges, high schools, and nursing schools. He was promised huge amounts of money to make these appearances, yet J.J. does not take payment for appearances that are not tied to his endorsement deals and contracts.

J.J. is not only a great football player, but also a positive role model for the youth. Instead of recklessly spending his days basking in his celebrity status, he spends his days training and trying to get better. He's disciplined and he deserves every accomplishment he has achieved so far. He is a wonderful example of not letting fame get to one's head, but instead maintaining the hunger as if he's still trying to earn his spot on an NFL roster.

Chapter 5:

Philanthropic/Charitable Acts

J.J. has made quite an impact off the field in his young career as a professional football player. He has founded and serves on the board for the Justin J. Watt Foundation. The foundation provides great opportunities to the youth, who aspire to leverage their time in after-school athletic programs.

Not only does the foundation help children to learn proper skills in athletics, but it also provides them the opportunity to develop life skills that will serve them in all aspects of life. They are able to learn character traits, such as leadership, work ethic, self-belief, and accountability, in a safe environment with other children their age. The foundation is currently involved in both Texas and Wisconsin.

J.J. has also held a charity softball game in the Greater Houston area. His J.J. Watt Charity Classic was held in Sugar Land, Texas and raised more than a quarter of a million dollars to help fund the after-school athletic programs with which his foundation works. The charity softball game featured some local celebrities and allowed J.J. to reconnect with the baseball roots that he left in Pewaukee High School.

Not all of J.J.'s charitable works are planned; however, as he is also known for his spontaneous acts of kindness. One such instance involves J.J. stopping by a little-league football practice in which he gave an impromptu motivational speech about how to become the best football player you can be and how to excel in other aspects of life. He openly shares his story and his struggles in the hope of inspiring the youth to pursue their dreams and make a difference in this world.

Chapter 6:

Legacy, Potential & Inspiration

While J.J.'s football career, hopefully, still has many years remaining, there is no doubt that he has already developed a legacy. His ability to dominate a football game is just one aspect in this legacy, as his ability to connect with fans is one of his greatest skills. He makes it a point to be relatable and not use his fame and fortune to corrupt his character.

Furthermore, J.J.'s hard working blue-collar attitude makes him a perfect fit for the Houston Texans organization. The team has not enjoyed much success during its short history, and it was not until J.J. arrived that the team was even able to make the postseason for the first time.

Not that J.J. is bigger than the team by any means, as the roster had been developed through the years, positioning themselves for the opportunity. However, J.J. does represent a new era and a renewed sense of hope within the fan base. To the people of Houston, he is a superhero. He's celebrated everywhere he goes.

He is already considered as one of the greatest players in franchise history, and his case will only continue to grow as he keeps putting up these productive seasons. However, J.J. values winning above all and doesn't focus on his individual statistics as much as many other elite level defensive players. Whether it be offensive shortcomings, special teams mistakes, or miscommunication amongst the team's defensive backs, J.J. covers for his teammates and doesn't find satisfaction in putting up massive numbers in a loss. He is truly a great team player, which is why his teammates love working and training with him.

J.J. has truly gained the respect of his colleagues and even his opponents. His opponents fear him, saying that he has a predatory mindset – something that makes him a dangerous player. He's passionate about what he does, and he puts all his emotions and focus into the game.

When you watch J.J. play, you can feel his passion, his hunger, and his desire to win. He wants to excel, and he wants to be the best at what he does. He's so good that his coach even lets him decide where to position in the line-up.

J.J. is serious about the game, but he's also playful. After he scored a touchdown, he did the "nae nae" dance along with his two other teammates, which amused many NFL fans. Although many football experts think he should stick to defense, J.J. thinks of expanding his horizons and went offense, occasionally, during his games in the 2015 season. After all, he used to be a tight end, before he switched to defensive end. Ziggy Hood of the Jacksonville Jaguars made a joke that the only thing that's holding J.J. back from being the best tight end in football is that he's trying to become the best defensive player ever.

The city of Houston is obsessed with J.J. Watt. Each time he does something awesome and amazing, the song "Turn

Down for What" comes on, and the fans scream, dance, and celebrate him. J.J. said in an interview that whenever his home stadium plays that song and the crowd goes wild, he feels electricity through his body. He goes nuts, and he feels like he's transported to a different world.

J.J. loves what he's doing, and he is a perfect example of a person who is dedicated to his work. He's as passionate as Michael Jordan is to basketball and Michael Jackson was to performing. He is a dominant player, and he is breaking records. What makes J.J. fascinating is that he's someone who still continues to work hard, even when he's already breaking records. He does not slack, not even for a day. He has a busy daily schedule during the season, but during the off season, he's busy with his endorsement deals and with his training.

J.J. is everywhere – on the red carpet, in award shows, on the magazine covers, and on television features. He even had a guest appearance at Jimmy Kimmel Live. He said that he's living the life that he has always dreamed of living because of all his hard work. J.J. saw how his parents worked hard when he was young, and this inspired him to do the same.

His parents, particularly his father, instilled the value of excellence in him at a very young age. His mother also made him do homework during summertime, and this taught him to always be one step ahead and to go the extra mile. J.J. is known for saying, "If you make minimum effort, you'll reap minimum results. If you want it, you have to get it."

While everyone else is sleeping or playing video games, he's working hard in the gym, trying to get himself into the perfect shape. He loves to train, and he loves every part of the training. His coaches believe his work ethic, his attitude, and his willingness to learn something new sets him apart from most other players. He has the desire to be great and is not afraid to make the necessary sacrifices.

J.J. believes that hard work is the key to his success, and he makes sure to maximize each day that he has. Whether it is in the weight room, on the practice field, or eating the right foods in the kitchen, J.J. has made it a point to commit his life to becoming the best, most impactful person he can be, both on and off the field.

He believes that being a superstar athlete is comparable to being a superhero. He is aware that little kids are looking up to him, and he wants to be a great example and an inspiration to them. He wants to inspire kids all over the world to work hard and pursue their own dreams. A lot of people in his hometown are proud of his achievements, including his former teammates and his teachers.

For J.J., his family is his inspiration. In fact, his grandfather is his greatest fan, and his parents are extremely proud of what he has achieved. At a young age of 26, J.J. Watt is now the NFL's number 1 football player, with a very bright future ahead of him.

Conclusion

I hope this book was able to help you gain inspiration from the story of J.J. Watt, one of the best players currently playing in the National Football League. At the same time, he is one of the nicest guys outside the gridiron, willing to help teammates and give back to fans. Last but not least, he's remarkable for remaining simple and firm with his principles, in spite of his immense popularity.

The rise and fall of a star is often the cause for much wonder, but most stars have an expiration date. In football, once a star player reaches his mid- to late-thirties, it is often time to contemplate retirement. What will be left in people's minds about that fading star? In J.J. Watt's case, people will remember how he led his team in their journey towards the playoffs. He will be remembered as the guy who plucked his team from obscurity, helped them build their image, and honed his own image along the way.

J.J. has also inspired so many people, because he is the star who never failed to look back, who paid his dues forward by helping thousands of less-fortunate youth find their inner light through sports and education. And another thing that stands out in J.J.'s history is the fact that he never forgot where he came from. As soon as he had the capacity to give back, he poured what he had straight back to those who needed it, and he continues to do so to this day.

Hopefully, you learned some great things about J.J. in this book and are able to apply some of the lessons that you've learned to your own life! Good luck in your own journey!

CPSIA information can be obtained
at www.ICGtesting.com
Printed in the USA
BVHW041105091218
535165BV00019B/610/P

9 781508 437987